WANDERLUST
TORONTO TRAVEL GUIDE
WITH NIAGARA FALLS, TOBERMORY, MUSKOKA, AND OTTAWA

D1798367

TORONTO
TRAVEL GUIDE

DIANA POLSKA

INTRODUCTION

wan·der·lust

noun

Wanderlust, literally "desire for wandering" is a strong desire for or impulse to wander or travel and explore the world.

Anyone with *wanderlust* is infected with the travel bug and has a strong desire to travel the world. *Wanderlusters* understand that that life is short and one of their main missions in life is to see what this beautiful world offers.

Wanderlust for Toronto? This is the best travel guide for you! Written by a Toronto expert that knows the city like the back of her hand. With this Toronto travel guide, you'll know exactly what to see and where to wander because "not all those who wander are lost."

Many Toronto city guides provide in-depth, but overwhelming details about the city that is irrelevant for first-time visitors or those that have a limited amount of time and only want to see the best of what the beautiful city of Toronto offers. If you're only visiting for a few days or a week, this Toronto travel guide is all you need to see the best of the city.

The absolute best cafes, restaurants, shopping, attractions, parks and neighborhoods are listed, described from an experienced local's perceptive.

Toronto Travel Guide includes destinations worthy of a multi-day or day trip that are only several hours away from Toronto such as Niagara Region (Niagara Falls, Niagara-on-the-Lake), Tobermory, Muskoka, and Ottawa.

The author has lived in Toronto for 30 years and is considered a Toronto Travel Expert. She has a great passion for good food, good coffee (and wine), good company, and most importantly good travel.

Table of Contents

WHY VISIT TORONTO?

Canada's commercial capital, Toronto is the most populated city in Canada, and one of the most populated cities in North America. Toronto is considered one of the most multicultural and cosmopolitan cities in the world. Toronto is commonly referred to as a "smaller version" of New York City.

Toronto is a global city, one of the world's most important cities. A global city runs the global economy, sets the global agenda, shapes the global culture and the global fashions. The Toronto Stock Exchange is the world's seventh-largest stock exchange by market capitalization.

Toronto ranks as the third largest production center for film and television after Los Angeles and New York, sharing the nickname "Hollywood North" with Vancouver. Hollywood loves Toronto and due to Toronto's diverse architecture, many TV shows, and movies are shot in Toronto even if they appear to be set in

US cities because Toronto resembles parts of New York City, Chicago, Washington, D.C., and Boston.

Several popular movies filmed in Toronto include *Mean Girls* (2004), *Cruel Intentions* (1999), *American Psycho* (2000), *X-Men* (2000), *Good Will Hunting* (1997), *Honey* (2003), *How to Lose a Guy in 10 Days* (2003), *My Big Fat Greek Wedding* (2002), *New York Minute* (2004), *Pixels* (2015), *Suicide Squad* (2016), *The Vow* (2012).

Several popular TV shows filmed in Toronto include *The Real Housewives of Toronto*, *Suits*, *Lost Girl*, *Covert Affairs*, *Orphan Black*, *Hannibal*, *Degrassi*, *Ready or Not*, and *Goosebumps*.

Toronto has low crime rates and has a reputation as one of the safest major cities in North America. Toronto is always ranked high in lists of the world's best cities and the world's most livable cities by several publications and surveys such as *The Economist*, *Economist Intelligence Unit*, *Mercer Quality of Life Survey*, and *Monocle Quality of Life Survey*.

A resident of Toronto is called a "Torontonian." Toronto has been nicknamed, "The 6ix," by famous Torontonian, Drake, because of Toronto's six areas (Old Toronto,

Scarborough, East York, North York, Etobicoke, and York).

A typical Torontonian loves their city regardless of the noise, traffic, and high cost of living. Torontonians are friendly and polite although usually rushed during the workweek.

Torontonians typically dress "stylish casual" although the style of dress varies a lot depending on the city's neighborhoods and districts. Those who work in the Financial District dress sharp while other dress simple and understated. Torontonians typically avoid dressing too trendy or flashy.

Torontonians love coffee. Torontonians that are "coffee snobs" only drink coffee from the best cafes in Toronto and don't typically like Tim Hortons coffee.

Torontonians love brunch and can be found at popular brunch restaurants on Saturdays and Sundays.

Torontonians are highly supportive of their baseball team, the Toronto Blue Jays. You will commonly find Torontonians wearing the Toronto Blue Jays hat or jersey shirt. Torontonians also support their hockey team, Toronto Maple Leafs and their basketball team, The Toronto Raptors.

A typical Torontonian is a trendsetter that thinks outside the box, embraces diversity, and is interested in international travel and contributing to a better world.

ARCHITECTURE

Toronto is composed of many high-rises within the downtown area referred to as Old Toronto. Toronto's buildings vary in design and age with many of the city's older buildings adopting designs from the British Empire, such as Georgian, Victorian, and Edwardian architecture, while many others are modern, elegant, shiny all-glass skyscrapers particularly within the Financial District.

Several particularly gorgeous buildings are designed by world-renowned architects. Allen Lambert Galleria at Brookfield Place was designed by architect Santiago Calatrava and is composed of steel arches creating a forest-like canopy over the pedestrian walkway. Calatrava also designed The Oculus at the World Trade Center in New York City. Daniel Libeskind designed the crystal-like sharp projection of the Royal Ontario Museum. Will Alsop has designed the table-like structure supported by brightly-colored, angled steel columns for the Sharp Centre for Design which is part of the Ontario College of Art and Design.

The Australian architect John Andrews designed the CN Tower that shapes the Toronto's distinctive skyline just like many other structures define a world-class city skyline: Sydney's Opera House, New York's Empire State Building, and London's Palace of Westminster.

Several architects collaborated on Toronto's Union Station. Designed in the Beaux-Arts style, it's a significant hub in Canada's transportation network—a primary railway station and part of the Toronto subway system (TTC).

FESTIVALS

The Toronto International Film Festival (TIFF) is a prestigious annual film festival held in the month of September celebrating the international film industry.

Danforth avenue (known as Greektown) is home to the annual "Taste of the Danforth" festival, Canada's largest street festival, held in August.

Toronto's Caribbean Carnival (also known as Caribana) takes place from mid-July to early August of every summer at Toronto's Lake Shore Boulevard.

One of the largest events in the city, Pride Week takes place in late June and is one of the largest LGBT festivals in the world.

The Canadian National Exhibition ("The Ex") is held annually at Exhibition Place from mid-August to early September, and it is the oldest annual fair in the world.

ATTRACTIONS

The two best museums and top attractions in Toronto are the Royal Ontario Museum and the Art Gallery of Ontario. The Royal Ontario Museum (ROM) is a museum of world culture and natural history. The Art Gallery of Ontario contains an extensive collection of Canadian, European, African and contemporary artwork, and regularly hosts exhibits from museums and galleries all over the world.

The Gardiner Museum of ceramic art is entirely devoted to displaying ceramics and contains more than 2,900 ceramic works from Asia, the Americas, and Europe.

The city is also home to other prominent art galleries and museums including the Ontario Science Centre, the Bata Shoe Museum, Textile Museum of Canada, Museum of Contemporary

Canadian Art (MOCCA), Aga Khan Museum, and Spadina House.

The Toronto Zoo is the largest zoo in Canada, home to over 5,000 animals. It has one of the most taxonomically diverse collections of animals on display of any zoo.

The city's major sports venues include the Air Canada Centre, Rogers Centre (formerly SkyDome), Ricoh Coliseum, and BMO Field.

Toronto has numerous ballet and dance companies, opera companies, symphony orchestras and a host of theaters. The city is home to the National Ballet of Canada, the Canadian Opera Company, the Toronto Symphony Orchestra, the Canadian Electronic Ensemble, and the Canadian Stage Company. Notable performance venues include the Four Seasons Centre for the Performing Arts, Roy Thomson Hall, the Princess of Wales Theatre, the Royal Alexandra Theatre, Massey Hall, the Toronto Centre for the Arts, the Elgin and Winter Garden Theatres and the Sony Centre for the Performing Arts.

The Entertainment District has all the most popular tourist attractions as well as many nightclubs, major theaters, and sports centers. The district is where the Toronto International Film Festival takes place every September. The area is home to the TIFF Bell Lightbox, Air

Canada Centre, Rogers Centre, Royal Alexandra Theatre, CN Tower, Metro Toronto Convention Centre, and Ripley's Aquarium of Canada. The area has some of the most well-reviewed, sophisticated, and popular restaurants and sports bars in the city.

SHOPPING

Toronto is a big city with many shopping districts with upscale boutiques, chain stores, malls, and independent shops.

One of the largest malls in Canada with hundreds of stores, the Eaton Centre has become known a tourist attraction. Visitors can spend hours roaming around several floors.

Bloor-Yorkville is an affluent shopping district with a mix of upscale boutiques and brand names stores located mainly on Bloor Street, Yorkville Avenue, Cumberland Street. Canada's most exclusive shopping street is Mink Mile (Bloor Street between Yonge Street and Avenue Road), ranked one of the most expensive shopping streets in the world.

Queen Street West is a hip shopping street, ranked one of the coolest neighborhoods in the world by *Vogue* magazine. There are numerous upscale as well as eclectic shops and clothing boutiques.

Toronto PATH is an underground walkway and shopping complex that is more than 30-kilometres long. According to the *Guinness World Records*, PATH is the largest underground shopping complex in the world. PATH links to many major buildings and provides an easy way to get somewhere in the city without enduring the snow or cold in the winter, and the heat and humidity in the summer.

FOOD AND DRINK

Toronto's food scene is top-notch—a foodie's paradise. As Toronto is so multicultural there is plenty of variety and numerous phenomenal restaurants.

St. Lawrence Market was ranked one of the world's best food market by National Geographic in the book *Food Journeys Of A Lifetime*. You can purchase locally-produced products and try new foods.

Upscale casual dining Canadian restaurant chains found in Canada's larger cities such as *Cactus Club Café*, *Milestones*, and *Earl's Kitchen and Bar* have great food for any occasion.

Canadians love coffee. Canada has the most Starbucks locations per person in the world. That's more than Starbucks has in its home country, the U.S.

Tim Hortons is a popular Canadian coffee franchise and many Canadians typically ordering a "Double-Double" (coffee with two creams and two sugars) and Timbits. *Second Cup Coffee Co.* and *Balzac's Coffee Roasters* are both Canadian coffee companies with cafes across the country.

BeaverTails are a must-try Canadian pastry shaped to resemble a beaver's tail with a selection of toppings.

LCBO is a retailer of alcoholic beverages throughout Toronto and Ontario. It's one of the world's largest buyers and retailers of beverage alcohol offering liquor, wine, and beer.

BEST OF TORONTO

BEST NEIGHBORHOODS

Toronto (The 6ix) is composed of six areas (Old Toronto, Scarborough, East York, North York, Etobicoke, and York). Many distinctive neighborhoods make up Toronto and the city's unofficial nickname is "the city of neighborhoods." There are 240 official and unofficial neighborhoods within the city's boundaries. For administrative purposes, the City of Toronto divides the city into 140 neighborhoods. The best neighborhoods in Toronto offer top-notch restaurants, cafes, shopping, entertainment, and nightlife.

Fashion District

The Fashion District is the area between Bathurst Street and Spadina Avenue on Queen and King Street West. King Street West contains some of the city's best and most trendy restaurants, nightclubs, shops, salons, and spas. Get your hair done, manicure and pedicure (or gentleman manicure/pedicure) at the elegant beauty salon, *Her Majesty's Pleasure*. Pick up some artisan *Soma* chocolates at the boutique located on the street. *Lee*, named after Susur Lee, is a stylish restaurant on King Street West known for creative Asian fusion. Susur Lee is an internationally acclaimed celebrity chef that owns several other restaurants in the city. He is well known for his dish **Singapore Slaw**. **WVRST** is a swanky restaurant with a German beer hall vibe that offers sausages, fries, and craft brews. There are several rooftop patios such as **Lavelle** and the exclusive **Thompson Toronto** rooftop which provide stunning views of the entire city skyline. **Chill Ice House** is Canada's largest ice lounge open all year offering vodka cocktails, wine, and other drinks. **BarChef** offers innovative cocktail using molecular mixology. Canada's Walk of Fame acknowledges the achievements of successful and famous Canadians, with a series of stars on designated blocks of sidewalks along King Street and Simcoe Street. Queen Street West is a hip shopping street, ranked one of the coolest neighborhoods in the world by *Vogue* magazine.

Distillery District

Once an alcohol processing center, the Distillery District is a National Historic Site of Canada that contains numerous cafés, restaurants, and shops housed within heritage buildings. It is the largest collection of Victorian-era industrial architecture in North America. It's a beautiful area for walking around, shopping or having a bite to eat and a beverage at a patio restaurant. During Christmas season, the Distillery District become a beautifully lit Christmas Market. *Soma* chocolate factory has a viewing area and offers inventive treats from chocolate bars to spicy cocoa. *Balzac's Coffee Roasters* is a beautiful café in the Distillery District. The Canadian coffee chain was named after the famous French novelist and famed coffee drinker Honoré de Balzac. *Cluny Bistro* and *El Catrin* are the Distillery District's most well-reviewed stylish restaurants. *Mill St. Brew Pub* is a micro-brewery with an on-site brewery that produces small batch seasonals. Visit nearby St. Lawrence Market which was named one of the world's best food market by *National Geographic* as well as the Gooderham Flatiron Building, a historic landmark.

Entertainment District

The Entertainment District has all the most popular tourist attractions as well as many nightclubs, major theaters, and sports centers. The area is home to the Air Canada Centre, Rogers Centre, Royal Alexandra Theatre, TIFF Bell Lightbox, CN Tower, Metro Toronto Convention Centre, and Ripley's Aquarium of Canada. The area has some of the most well-reviewed, sophisticated, and popular restaurants and sports bars in the city such as *360 The Restaurant at the CN Tower*, *The Fifth Grill*, *Byblos*, *Fune Japanese Restaurant*, *Alo Restaurant*, *Luma*, *Azure Restaurant*, *Aria Ristorante*, *Real Sports Bar*, *e11even*, and *Soco Kitchen*. *Steam Whistle Brewing*, voted "best beer in Toronto" and "best microbrewery in Toronto," produces a premium pilsner lager in distinctive packaging. *Crocodile Rock* is a popular spot for drinks and has a large rooftop patio. *The Fifth Social* is a landmark in the Toronto social scene; a stylish ex-loft with an upscale atmosphere for nightlife. *Second City* is an improv and sketch comedy theater with nightly shows.

Harbourfront

Harbourfront is a neighborhood on Toronto's waterfront located around Queens Quay West. There numerous waterside restaurants, cafes, and pubs. *Amsterdam BrewHouse* is a popular lakeside brewery that pairs craft beer with local foods. *Boxcar Social* has a lakeside terrace and offers coffee and selection of alcohol. Harbourfront Centre is a great place to stroll and people-watch as well as enjoy a beverage, lunch, or dinner. *BeaverTails* is a popular Canadian-based chain of delicious fried dough pastries resembling a beaver's tail. The restaurant is located right by Harbourfront Centre. Harbourfront Centre works with numerous community organizations, and hosts thousands of annual events such as theater, dance, literature, music, film, visual arts or craft.

Yonge and Eglington
Midtown Toronto's central neighborhood is Yonge and Eglinton. There are many excellent restaurants, cafes and boutiques in the area, most notably **Himalayan Java House** and **North 44** restaurant. There are several well-reviewed Italian restaurants such as **Grazie Ristorante**, **La Vecchia Ristorante**, and **Amore Trattoria**. Located on Mount Pleasant Road, **The Homeway** is a cozy brunch spot. The upscale neighborhood of Midtown Toronto and heading North until York Mills comprise some of the most affluent residences in the city. For wanderlust travelers interested in exploring Toronto's wealthiest residential neighborhoods and admiring multimillion-dollar mansions, drive or wander through The Bridal Path, Rosedale, Forest Hill, and Lawrence Park. The Bridle Path mansions were used in the filming of several movies. The mansion at 11 High Point Road was Regina's house in the movie *Mean Girls* (2004). The mansion at 68 The Bridle Path was the home of one of the Olsen twins in the

movie *It Takes Two* (1995) and was in an episode of *Suits*.

Bloor-Yorkville
Bloor-Yorkville is an affluent neighborhood with a mix of upscale boutiques and brand names stores located mainly on Bloor Street, Yorkville Avenue, and Cumberland Street. Canada's most exclusive shopping street is Mink Mile (Bloor Street between Yonge Street and Avenue Road), ranked one of the most expensive shopping streets in the world. Get a facial at one of the best spas in Toronto at **Novo Spa**. Make a stop at **Holt Renfrew**, Canada's leading high-end department store and the flagship **Harry Rosen**, a Canadian retail chain of high-end menswear. There are numerous excellent cafes in the area such as **Goldstruck Coffee**, **Sorry Coffee Co**, **Crema Coffee Co.** and **Nespresso Café**. The best restaurants in the area are **Sassafraz** which offers French-inspired Canadian cuisine, and **La Société** which offer French bistro fare in a posh space with a huge stained-glass ceiling. **Planta** is an innovative plant-based restaurant offering internationally-inspired meatless dishes served in a stylish setting. **The One Eighty** offers beautiful views of the city from the 51st floor and has a good

drinks menu of seasonal cocktails, martinis, champagne, wine, beer, and spirits.

Yonge Street

Yonge Street is one of Toronto's busiest streets. Starting from the intersection of Yonge and Bloor, take a stroll down Yonge Street Southbound toward the waterfront. The street runs vertical to some of the most popular and vibrant streets in downtown Toronto such as Dundas, Queen, Richmond, Adelaide, King, Wellington, and Front. It takes approximately half an hour to walk from Yonge-Bloor down to Front Street. *Wish* restaurant offers brunch, lunch, dinner and drinks in a stylish surrounding. *7 West Cafe* is Toronto's most recognized names in comfort dining. The hideaway takes over all three floors of an old Victorian townhome and is open 24 hours a day, 7 days a week, offering drinks, coffee, or food. *Ethiopian House* restaurant offers delicious Ethiopian dishes and share platters eaten by hand, and has a coffee roasting ceremony. *Signs Restaurant* is a unique restaurant offering Canadian fare that is staffed with deaf servers and visitors must order in sign language from a cheat sheet without speaking. *Onoir* is a two-hour dining experience in a pitch-black room that is supposed to heighten the senses.

Yonge-Dundas Square

Yonge-Dundas Square in the heart of the city is a smaller version of New York Times Square. The square is one of the busiest gathering spots in Toronto and typically has entertaining street performers and musicians on the weekends. CF Toronto Eaton Centre is also located in the square. A celebrated Canadian landmark, Eaton Centre has a striking glass galleria and iconic "Flight Stop" geese, a permanent sculptural installation. *Richmond Station* is a well-reviewed and popular restaurant offering seasonal cuisine. *Baton Rouge Steakhouse & Bar* at the Eaton Centre is a Canadian restaurant chain, famous for their baby back ribs, Sterling Silver steaks, and grilled catch of the day. *Sunset Grill* is a Canadian restaurant chain known for its traditional breakfast and brunch menu. *The Senator*, opened in 1929, is a Toronto landmark. It's a popular spot for a classic breakfast and brunch.

Nathan Phillips Square

Nearby Yonge-Dundas Square is Nathan Phillips Square, the city's iconic main square with its reflecting pool, Toronto sign in front of the New City Hall. The reflecting pool converts into a skating rink in the wintertime. There is an elevated walkway that is a good place for photographs of the square and the surrounding city. *Nota Bene,* only a few minutes away from Nathan Phillips Square, is a hip restaurant offering upscale, creative Canadian dishes in a sleek, contemporary setting. *Bannock* is steps away from Nathan Phillips Square and serves the best in Canadian comfort food for brunch, lunch, or dinner.

Financial District
The Financial District is the financial heart of Canada and contains modern and elegant architecture. It is home to numerous banks, corporate headquarters, legal and accounting firms, insurance companies and stockbrokers, advertising agencies and marketing companies. A high concentration of banks and brokerage firms are located on Bay Street. The Financial District has some of the most polished and swanky restaurants in the city. *Canoe* is a sophisticated restaurant on the 54th floor with a stunning view of the city offering creative Canadian cuisine. *Bymark* offers continental dishes and cocktails in an elegant dining room and on a large patio. *Drake One Fifty* is a stylish restaurant that offers upscale Canadian dishes. *VOLOS* is an upscale Greek restaurant in a contemporary setting. *The Gabardine* offers

hearty comfort food in a cozy yet elegant setting. *Cactus Club Cafe* is a Canadian casual dining restaurant chain. *Beerbistro* is a lively, elegant spot that offers a long list of brews and specializes in cooking with beer. *The Keg Steakhouse* is a Canadian chain of steakhouse restaurants that offers classic steak and seafood dishes—one of the most popular locations in Toronto is the one at York Street. *Reservoir Lounge* is a hip nightlife spot with live jazz, swing, and blues 5-nights a week and offers late-night tapas and cocktails.

Kensington Market

Located beside Toronto's Chinatown is Kensington Market. Designated a National Historic Site of Canada, it's an eccentric neighborhood filled with thrift and vintage stores, restaurants, and independent coffee shops. There are many food stores selling a variety of meats, fish and produce as well as several bakeries, and cheese shops. *Vegetarian Haven* offers vegan Asian-influenced dishes made with mock meats. *Urban Herbivore* has lots of healthy and organic vegan options such as nutritious salads, sandwiches, and soups. *The Dirty Bird Chicken + Waffles* serves fried chicken and waffles with a Canadian twist. *Jimmy's Coffee* is a popular Toronto coffee shop with several locations—the coffee shop at Kensington Market has an industrial living room vibe and back area has bookcases filled with leather-bound tomes.

BEST ATTRACTIONS

Toronto is cosmopolitan city offering numerous attractions for everyone. Most of the top attraction are within walking distance of each other in downtown Toronto and several others are easily accessible by using the subway system.

Brookfield Place
One of the most spectacular interiors in Toronto is found at Brookfield Place on Bay Street, within the Financial District. Allen Lambert Galleria, designed by Santiago Calatrava, is composed of steel arches creating a forest-like canopy over the pedestrian walkway and connects to the intertwining steel arches at Sam Pollock Square. Head downstairs from Allen Lambert Galleria to the PATH underground shops, one of the world's largest underground shopping complexes with 30 km (19 miles) of shops, restaurants, and cafes. The CN Tower, Ripley's Aquarium of Canada, and Rogers Centre are connected via an enclosed elevated walkway, called the SkyWalk. Brookfield Place is also home to the Hockey Hall of Fame.

Royal Bank Plaza

Royal Bank Plaza, located in the Financial District, is a photogenic building due to its unusual angles and the way in which light reflects and bounces off the gold-bronze colored building with its 14,000 windows. The glass covering the skyscraper is colored with over 2,500 ounces of 24K gold, valued at approximately 1 million dollars. No one bothers to break and steal the glass because putting gold into glass makes the gold worthless.

CN Tower

The CN Tower is Toronto's tallest and most defining landmark. There is a glass floor that visitors can walk across and stand on. The CN Tower also has a revolving 360 restaurant, a great spot to dine while taking in the city's panorama. EdgeWalk, the world's highest full-circle, hands-free walk offers visitors a walk along the Tower's ledge to experience breathtaking views of the city below. EdgeWalk is open from spring through until fall and is closed for the winter.

Ripley's Aquarium Of Canada

Ripley's Aquarium Of Canada is an aquarium that is adjacent to the CN Tower. There are several aquatic exhibits including a walk-through tank. The exhibits hold over 13,500 exotic sea and freshwater specimens from more than 450 species. One of the most well-liked exhibits is the color changing displays with five species of jellyfish that include: pacific sea nettle, moon jelly, spotted jelly, and upside-down jelly.

Rogers Centre
Adjacent to the CN Tower is Rogers Centre, a massive domed sports arena. The roof slides back, allowing it to be opened during the summer. Rogers Centre is a venue for every kind of sport, baseball, and football, as well as for rock and pop concerts. The center also offers one hour guided tours with a behind-the-scenes look at the facility.

King Street West
King Street West comes to life in the evenings and is Toronto's version of New York's Broadway. King Street West has major theater productions, musicals, concerts, and other performing arts such as Royal Alexandra Theatre, Roy Thomson Hall, Princess of Wales Theatre, Toronto Symphony Orchestra, and TIFF Bell Lightbox. There are also all kinds of restaurants and bars for socializing.

Graffiti Alley

Graffiti Alley in The Fashion District is south of Queen Street West between Spadina Avenue and Portland Street beginning at Rush Lane. The kilometer-long alley is full of gorgeous, vibrant, and colorful murals and graffiti.

Art Gallery of Ontario (AGO)

The AGO is one of the largest galleries in North America. The entrance is on Dundas Street near McCaul Street. It has a collection of more than 80,000 works spanning the first century to the present day. It has a large collection of Canadian art, works from the Renaissance and the Baroque eras, European art, African and Oceanic art, and a modern and contemporary collection.

Royal Ontario Museum (ROM)

The ROM is Canada's largest museum and one of the largest museums in North America. It is located just to the west of Yorkville, at the intersection of Bloor and Avenue Road. The ROM has more than six million items spanning diverse collections of world culture and natural history. The museum contains collections of dinosaurs, minerals and meteorites, Mesopotamian and African art, Art of East Asia, European history, and Canadian history. It houses the world's largest collection of fossils from the Burgess Shale with more than 150,000 specimens. The museum also contains an extensive collection of design and fine arts.

Ontario Science Centre
Ontario Science Centre offers hundreds of interactive exhibits of science and technology. There are exhibits dedicated to sports, communication, the Human Body and The Living Earth. There is also a planetarium and an OMNIMAX movie theater.

Toronto Zoo
The Toronto Zoo is the largest zoo in Canada, home to over 5,000 animals. It has one of the most taxonomically diverse collections of animals on display of any zoo. The zoo is in Toronto's east end district of Scarborough.

Canada's Wonderland
Canada's Wonderland, located in Vaughan, ON., is about a 40-minute drive north of Toronto. It's one of the most visited seasonal amusement parks in North America, open from May to September. Canada's Wonderland is ranked third in the world by number of roller coasters and has North America's greatest variety of roller coasters. The 330-acre amusement park includes a 20-acre water park.

Casa Loma

Casa Loma is a Gothic Revival castle built in 1911 by Sir Henry Mill Pellatt, complete with gardens, turrets, stables, an elevator, secret passages, a library, a dining room to seat 100, and an indoor swimming pool. The castle was designed by renowned Toronto architect E.J. Lennox. It has 98 rooms covering 64,700 square feet.

BAPS Shri Swaminarayan Mandir

The Hindu temple is a gorgeous, meticulously built place of worship consisting of 24,000 pieces of hand-carved Italian Carrara marble, Turkish limestone, and Indian pink stone. It's located at 61 Claireville Drive, approximately 40-minute drive from downtown Toronto.

Hockey Hall of Fame

Hockey Hall of Fame is a museum and a hall of fame located at the corner of Front and Yonge Street. It has exhibits about players, teams, NHL records, memorabilia and NHL trophies, including the Stanley Cup. The Great Hall, contains portraits and biographical information about every Hall of Fame honored member.

Union Station

Located on Front Street West, massive and magnificent Beaux-Arts style Union Station has been designated a National Historic Site of Canada and a Heritage Railway Station. The front entranceway opens onto the expansive ticket lobby. Intercity train services are provided by Via Rail and Amtrak, while commuter rail services are operated by GO Transit. The station is also connected to the Toronto Transit Commission (TTC) subway.

St. Lawrence Market

The St. Lawrence Market was ranked one of the world's best food markets by National Geographic. There are numerous produce and food stalls, restaurants, art exhibits and cooking classes. Try Toronto's signature dish—the famous peameal bacon sandwich at Carousel Bakery.

BEST RESTAURANTS

Toronto's food scene is top-notch—a foodie's paradise. There are so many phenomenal restaurants in Toronto that it's extremely hard to narrow down the best restaurants in Toronto. Therefore, the absolute best restaurants in Toronto are those that have been around for a long time and consistently offer quality and great service. While in Toronto, it's advised to check out Canadian-based restaurant chains such as Smoke's Poutinerie, Cora, Earls Kitchen, JOEY, The Keg, Kelsey's, Moxie's, Milestones, Pickle Barrel, and Cactus Club Café.

Mocha Mocha
Mocha Mocha is a casual dining restaurant serving brunch and a varied menu of global fare, from African stew to burritos to pasta. The restaurant is located on Danforth Avenue in the neighborhood known as Greektown.

Scaramouche
Scaramouche is arguably one of the best fine dining restaurants in Toronto. It offers sophisticated French haute cuisine in an upscale space with skyline views of Toronto. The

restaurant is in midtown Toronto near Casa Loma.

Lee

Lee restaurant, named after the owner Susur Lee, is a stylish restaurant on King Street West known for creative Asian fusion. Susur Lee is an internationally acclaimed celebrity chef that owns several other restaurants in the city. The restaurant's signature dish is the Singapore Slaw, an extravagant and colorful slaw consisting of 19 unique ingredients.

Fresh

Fresh is one of Toronto's leading modern vegetarian restaurants and offers made-to-order juice. The food is made daily in-house, from whole, natural ingredients. There are several locations throughout the city including Bloor Street West, Spadina Avenue, Queen Street West, and Eglington Avenue East.

360 The Restaurant at the CN Tower

The revolving 360 restaurant at the CN Tower offers regional Canadian fare and is a great spot to dine while taking in the city's panorama. CN Tower Wine Cellar was designated the "World's Highest" by Guinness World Records at 351 meters (1151 ft.). 360 Restaurant has received

Best of Award of Excellence for its wine list and has a varied, well-considered selection of wine. 360 Restaurant has been honored with the DiRoNA (Distinguished Restaurants of North America) Award of Excellence which is presented to restaurants across North America in recognition of their commitment to excellence in all areas including food, beverage, decor, and experience.

La Castile
Opened in 1968, the restaurant offers steak and seafood in spectacular and opulent castle-like setting of dark wood and stained glass. The restaurant is in Mississauga, about a 10-minute drive from the Toronto Pearson International Airport.

Old Spaghetti Factory
Opened in 1971, the iconic Spaghetti Factory was originally a blacksmith shop has an antique elevator, streetcar, original stained glass windows from Europe, gas lamps, an old carousel and several other intriguing antiques and artifacts. The classic dish to try is the spaghetti and meatballs.

Barbarian's Steak House

Suitable for special occasions, it's an old-school steakhouse considered by many older locals as a Toronto landmark. It's been open since 1959, offering a perfectly cooked steak in a romantic setting.

North 44

North 44 restaurant has been around for a long time. It's located on Yonge Street in North Toronto. It is an elegant and modern space offering a contemporary menu, extensive wine list, and impeccable service.

Canoe

A stylish, swanky restaurant on the 54th floor of the Toronto-Dominion Centre in the Financial District has a creative Canadian cuisine and exceptional views of the city. Food presentation is excellent and the service is unpretentious and professional.

George

George is a top-rated restaurant noted for its innovative "Toronto cuisine" devoted to making everything from scratch using fresh, seasonal and local ingredients where possible. George restaurant is the ultimate Toronto destination for an elevated food experience.

Jacobs & Co. Steakhouse

Jacobs & Co. is one of Toronto's most distinguished steakhouses. It's a restaurant where pro hockey players, celebrities, and businessmen enjoy top cuts of meat as well as the very best service.

The Senator

Opened in 1929, The Senator diner is a Toronto landmark. It's a popular spot for a classic breakfast and brunch. Its outdated décor remains from the original style and fixtures from 1948.

BEST CAFES

Toronto is filled with coffee lovers and there are plenty of top-notch independent coffee shops. There are several cat cafes where visitors can get a coffee and interact with cats. Of course, there is the popular coffee franchise, Tim Hortons, known for its coffee and doughnuts. Many typically order a "Double-Double" (coffee with two creams and two sugars). Second Cup Coffee Co. and Balzac's Coffee Roasters are both Canadian coffee shops with cafes across the city.

Himalayan Java House
Himalayan Java opened its first location in Kathmandu, Nepal, and the company has expanded and opened locations in various cities. Himalayan Java House in Toronto does exquisite latte art. The lattes are tasty and made from high-quality Nepali coffee beans. The interior is small, cramped, but cozy.

Cafe Belong
Cafe Belong is located in Evergreen Brick Works. The mochaccino and lattes are some of the best in the city served in an airy space with wraparound windows.

Dineen Coffee Co.

Dineen is a boutique coffee house at the corner of Yonge Street and Temperance Street in a historic building that is one of the oldest structures in Toronto. The stylish interior is impressive and elaborate and the café also offers an outdoor patio. A rotation of drip coffees are available daily, and there are known for their excellent lattes.

Te Aro

Ranked one of the best independent coffee shops in Toronto by numerous locals for a latte, flat white, cappuccino, cortado, espresso, and Americano.

Lit Expresso Bar

Lit Expresso Bar has several locations in Toronto and offers exceptional brewed coffee and cappuccinos that are smooth and rich.

de Mello Palheta

de Mello Palheta is a small café located in North Toronto near Yonge and Eglington. The flat white from the café is the best in the city.

Balzac's Coffee Roasters

Balzac's Coffee Roasters is a Canadian coffee chain with several locations in the city. It was named after the famous French novelist and famed coffee drinker Honoré de Balzac.

Sam James Coffee Bar (SJCB)
SJCB is ranked as one of the best independent coffee shops in the Toronto coffee scene and has many local fans. The espressos and lattes are smooth and creamy, many locals are don't even add any sugar. SJCB has several locations in Toronto.

Boxcar Social
Boxcar Social has several locations in Toronto, the most popular location in the summer is at Habourfront Centre which has a patio overlooking Lake Ontario. They offer a curated, rotating list of coffees from the best roasters in North America.

Snakes and Lattes
Snakes and Lattes is a board game café with a huge collection of board and card games plus light food and coffee with a focus on socializing with friends. Snakes and Lattes has been cited as the inspiration for the opening of many other board game cafes around the world.

BEST SHOPPING

Toronto has several excellent shopping districts. The Eaton Centre is a very popular tourist attraction and is always very busy but there are other excellent shopping malls. There are several leading Canadian brands such as Roots; Aritzia women's clothing; Le Chateau evening wear; Canada Goose parkas and jackets, Hudson's Bay iconic striped hats or scarves; Lululemon athletic wear; Mendocino dresses, Peace Collective streetwear t-shirts with phrases such as "Home is Toronto" and "Toronto vs Everybody".

Mink Mile

Mink Mile is Canada's most exclusive shopping districts within Yorkville, along Bloor Street West between Yonge Street and Avenue Road. Holt Renfrew and Harry Rosen are two flagship stores located on Mink Mile. Holt Renfrew is Canada's leading high-end department store. Harry Rosen is a Canadian retail chain of high-end menswear.

Queen Street West

Queen Street West was named the second coolest neighborhood in the world by Vogue magazine. The hip shopping street between Bathurst and Gladstone is home to some of the city's most trendy boutiques. There are numerous upscale as well as eclectic shops and clothing boutiques.

Yorkdale Shopping Centre
Yorkdale is a major retail shopping mall in Toronto containing numerous Canadian brand name stores such as Holt Renfrew, Hudson's Bay, Indigo Books and Music, Canada Goose, Harry Rosen, Lululemon Athletica, Le Chateau, Mendocino, Aritzia, and ALDO.

Square One Shopping Centre
Square One is the second largest shopping center in Canada and the largest shopping center in Ontario. Square One has numerous Canadian retailers such as Hudson's Bay, Canada's iconic chain of department stores, and flagship store Simons.

Vaughan Mills
Vaughan Mills is Toronto's premier outlet mall and contains the world's leading fashion and lifestyle brands. It is one of the largest shopping centers in Canada located adjacent to Canada's Wonderland.

Shops at Don Mills

Shops at Don Mills is an outdoor shopping center with numerous brand name shops and boutiques. It's located at Don Mills Road and Lawrence Avenue East.

Toronto PATH

Toronto PATH is an underground walkway and shopping complex that is more than 30-kilometres long. According to the Guinness World Records, PATH is the largest underground shopping complex in the world with 371,600 square meters (4,000,000 sq ft) of retail space. The stores are only open during weekday business hours. During the evenings and weekends, the walkways remain open but most of the stores are closed.

Winners

Winners is a chain of Canadian department stores offering brand-name goods (especially clothing) sold for less than the usual retail price. Winners has numerous locations in Toronto.

Canada Goose

Canada Goose, founded by Polish immigrant Sam Tick, is an arctic luxury apparel brand. It is world-famous for its down-filled jackets and parkas. It also offers vests, hats, gloves, shells and other apparel. The jackets and parkas have been worn by many celebrities and appeared in film and television. Moose Knuckles is its main competitor.

Soma
Soma Chocolate is a boutique artisan chocolatier in Toronto. It specializes in making chocolates directly from the cocoa bean and in small batches. The shop offers Fairtrade and organic chocolates from various parts of the world. The various shops around Toronto offer truffles, caramels, chocolate bars, chocolate desserts, and drinks.

Kitten and the Bear
Kitten and the Bear is a bespoke Toronto jam and scone shop and café. They also carry Sloane Tea to purchase, premium specialty teas in beautiful packaging made in Toronto.

Sugar Mountain
Sugar Mountain is Toronto's leading candy store offering high-quality bulk and imported candy, sugar-free choices, and the very best of Canadian candy. It has won the Best Candy Store in Toronto award by several local publications.

BEST PARKS

Toronto has more than 1,500 parks with numerous open spaces and 600 km of trails. The parks cover 8,000 hectares or roughly 13% of the city's land area. City parks have beaches, playgrounds, sports fields, gardens, conservatories, and ice rinks.

Toronto Island
Take a ferry from the Jack Layton Ferry Terminal and enjoy the city's largest parkland. You can have a picnic, bike or canoe around the island, or sun tan on the "clothing optional" beach called Hanlan's Point.

Allan Gardens Conservatory
Allen Gardens Conservatory is a major landmark in Toronto. It's a historic, cast-iron and glass domed greenhouse with a permanent collection of exotic plants and beautiful seasonal flower shows.

Scarborough Bluffs
The Scarborough Bluffs has been described as a "geological wonder" and a unique feature in North America. The Scarborough Bluffs run 14

kilometers from the foot of Victoria Park Avenue in the west to the mouth of Highland Creek in the east, reaching as high seventeen stories.

Guild Park and Gardens
Guild Park is about a 10-minute drive from Scarborough Bluffs. There are historic stone sculptures and arches and a promenade leading to the Scarborough Bluffs.

Sunnyside Park
Sunnyside Park is located at the west end of Toronto on the shore of Lake Ontario. Sunnyside has a boardwalk for pedestrians and the Martin Goodman Trail for cyclists. Sunnyside Café is a great place for a bite to eat during the summer months.

Edwards Garden
Edwards Gardens is adjacent to the Toronto Botanical Garden. The former estate garden has wildflowers, rhododendrons, perennials, and roses. Edwards Gardens is one of the several parks located along Toronto's ravines, many of which are connected by bike trails.

Riverdale Park

Riverdale park has a beautiful skyline view of Toronto. The park has recreational fields for soccer, baseball, as well as a swimming pool, tennis courts, outdoor hockey rink and a running track in the center. The park is connected to Riverdale Farm that is home to a variety of domestic farm animals. It has livestock, gardens and natural surroundings that reflect a typical, small Ontario farm of the late 19th to early 20th century.

Evergreen Brick Works
The Don Valley Brick Works is a former industrial site that opened in 1889 and was partly restored as a park and heritage site in 1996, with further restoration and reuse being completed in stages since then.

High Park
High Park spans 161 hectares (400 acres) with sporting facilities, cultural facilities, educational facilities, gardens, playgrounds and a zoo. The park is very busy in the spring during cherry blossoms season. During the summer months, the Canadian Stage Company company puts on selected Shakespearean plays in the park's amphitheater, an annual event called "Shakespeare in High Park."

Mount Pleasant Cemetery

Mount Pleasant Cemetery is ranked one of the world's most scenic cemeteries by several sources. With its rolling green hills, varied trees, flowers, elegant fountains, and grand mausoleums, it's regarded by nearby residents as a public park and during summer, there are many who stroll or jog in the cemetery. It the resting place for some of Canada's most famous citizens.

TRIPS FROM TORONTO

OTTAWA

Museums
Ottawa is packed with some of Canada's best museums and galleries including the Canadian War Museum, National Gallery of Canada, Canadian Nature Museum, National Aviation Museum, and Canada's Cold War Museum.

Parliament Hill
The Gothic Revival suite of buildings is the home of the Parliament of Canada. The Parliament of Canada is composed of three parts: the monarch, the Senate, and the House of Commons. Tickets for the tour are free from the building opposite the parliament building.

Rideau Canal
The Rideau Canal is a UNESCO World Heritage Site and is one of the world's largest skating rinks. January to late February is the ideal time to glide along the 7.8 kilometers (4.8 miles) of ice, which stretches from Ottawa's downtown core to Dows Lake.

Royal Canadian Mint

The headquarters of the Royal Canadian Mint is located in central Ottawa. The facility produces hand-crafted collector and commemorative coins, gold bullion coins, medals, and medallions. Visit the boutique to buy collectors coins or gifts. You can also take a guided tour to learn how coins are made.

Byward Market
The Byward Market is one of Canada's oldest and largest public markets. Within an area roughly four blocks square, you'll find cafés, specialty food shops, boutiques, restaurants, and pubs.

NIAGARA REGION

Niagara Falls
One of the seven natural wonders of the world, Niagara Falls is the collective name for three waterfalls that straddle the international border between Canada and the United States. Journey Behind the Falls to see the falls up close or zip line high above the falls with WildPlay's MistRider. The Bird Kingdom and Butterfly Conservatory are popular attractions in the area.

Niagara-on-the-Lake
Niagara-on-the-Lake is Canada's best food and wine destination. Most of the wineries in the region offer winery tours and experiences all year long. Some wineries also arrange private or group tours when booked in advance. The small town located on Queen Street is one of the most well-preserved 19th-century towns in the country.

TOBERMORY

Shipwreck Diving

Tobermory is famous for having shallow, easily accessible shipwrecks in Fathom Five National Marine Park and offers some of the best freshwater diving in Canada. There are over 20 historic shipwrecks submerged in clear, clean water. Some shipwrecks can be viewed without having to scuba as they are shallow enough to see via snorkeling and boat. If you don't dive or snorkel, you can see shipwrecks from a glass-bottom tour boat.

Bruce Peninsula National Park

The park has great hiking and semi-wilderness camping. The park has beautiful geological formations. Take the Bruce Trail to see the Grotto, a big cave on the shore carved out by the waves of Georgian Bay over thousands of years.

MUSKOKA

Winter Activities

Muskoka is a popular summer cottage destination for Torontonians being only about a two-hour drive from Toronto. However, aside from being great cottage country, there are many exciting traditional Canadian winter activities. Popular activities include dogsledding, ice fishing, skiing, snowshoeing, and ice skating on a 1.5 kilometers trail that winds through the Muskoka forest.

Torrance Barrens Dark-Sky Preserve

Torrance Barrens is a "dark-sky preserve" near Muskoka. Access to Torrance Barrens is off District Road 13 (Southwood Road). It's a great place for camping. There is an absence of light pollution at night, therefore it's a remarkable place to view stars and the Milky Way. At certain times of the year, you will be able to see the magical Northern Lights (Aurora Borealis).

ALGONQUIN PROVINCIAL PARK

Canoe Camping
Canoe camping is one of the most popular activities in the park. This wilderness experience is a canoe journey through the vast park, allowing the tourist to enjoy the interior of the park in ways inaccessible by any other means.

Wilderness Activities
Fishing, mountain biking, horseback riding, cross country skiing, and day hiking are popular activities for visitors to Algonquin Provincial Park. The park has 19 interpretive trails, ranging in length from 1 to 11.7 kilometers. Each trail comes with a trail guide.

RESOURCES

CITY GUIDES
Toronto
www.toronto.com

BlogTO Best of Toronto
www.blogto.com/toronto

Toronto Life
www.torontolife.com

Narcity Toronto
www.narcity.com/toronto

Toronto Wiki
http://wiki.wikito.org

RESTAURANTS
TripAdvisor Restaurants

www.tripadvisor.ca/Restaurants

Taste Toronto
www.tastetoronto.ca

BlogTO Find a Restaurant
www.blogto.com/restaurants

Toronto Life Where to Eat and Drink
www.torontolife.com/guides/restaurants

Dine.TO Category Restaurant Search
www.dine.to/toronto_restaurants.php

Toronto Food & Drink
www.toronto.com/food-drink

CAFES
TOcafes
www.tocafes.com

BlogTO Find a Café
www.blogto.com/cafes

Dine.TO Category Café Search
www.dine.to/toronto_cafes.php

SHOPPING

See Toronto Now Fabulous Shopping
www.seetorontonow.com/shopping

Bloor-Yorkville Shopping
www.bloor-yorkville.com/cat/shopping

Toronto Eaton Centre
www.cfshops.com/toronto-eaton-centre/stores.html

Yorkdale Shopping Centre
www.yorkdale.com

Vaughan Mills
www.vaughanmills.com

Square One Shopping Centre
www.shopsquareone.com

SPORTS
Sports and Entertainment
www.seetorontonow.com/category/sports-recreation

Toronto Blue Jays
www.toronto.bluejays.mlb.com

Toronto Maple Leafs

www.nhl.com/mapleleafs

Toronto Raptors
http://www.nba.com/raptors

Toronto FC
www.torontofc.ca

THEATRE
Theatre Calendar
www.toronto.com/theatre

Guide to the Best Shows
www.toronto-theatre.com

Arts, Theatre and Culture
www.seetorontonow.com/arts-theatre-culture

NIGHTLIFE
Club Crawlers
www.clubcrawlers.com

Club Zone Toronto
www.clubzone.com/toronto

See Toronto Now Bars and Nightlife
www.seetorontonow.com/bars-nightlife

Lightning Source UK Ltd.
Milton Keynes UK
UKOW06f1835310317
298065UK00006B/140/P